MESSAGES IN A BOTTLE
Inspirations in Poetic Prose

by Branch Isole

MESSAGES IN A BOTTLE
Inspirations in Poetic Prose
by Branch Isole

Printed in the United States of America

Library of Congress Control Number:
2004112989
ISBN   0-9747692-9-0

MANA'O PUBLISHING

Home of the VOYEURISTIC POET

PO Box 1696
Lahaina, HI 96767-1696

Order additional copies of this book at
www.manaopublishing.com

My poetry is inspired by the Hula.
The Hula is precise, sensual, sexual
and sophisticatedly raw as it tells a story.
I am a voyeur of the Hula for all its character.

The poems herein are short stories of
issues and emotions surrounding personal
responsibility choice and avoidance.
This is 'Voyeurism Poetry'.

Messages in a Bottle contains adult material and
language, some of which is sexual in nature.
It is intended for mature audiences only.

Contents

Introduction

In the 1950's it was common practice in many schools to require students to write. During those years at some point in most middle grade academic careers it was both the task and bane to have been asked or assigned to write an essay along the lines of "What I did on my summer vacation."

A summer's activities often proved to be interesting to recall, yet difficult to explain. The assignment always seemed more an exercise in tedium and embellishment in order to meet the required number of words, than relevant story retelling. It wasn't that the summer was boring, it required a grueling effort to get the words down on paper.

Looking back, those attempts at more than penmanship were opportunities to express creatively, both the real and imagined.

Everyone has a story to tell. Too often however, our children dismiss themselves and their value as individuals for an iconic emulation of the latest or most outrageous pop culture idolatry. This is not a new phenomenon; it is the way of our world. How we express it has changed. No longer does there seem to be an individual identity built upon a young person's discovery of him or herself and their world.

It has become easier to merely copy an existing entity with added emphasis on being more explicit, perverse or deviant in behavior exhibited lock step with the 'in your face' attitude of reality TV.

Today, youngsters from the earliest stages of understanding are often encouraged and/or desire themselves to become a branded identity prepackaged behind the scenes by agents and gurus regardless of the short lived possibilities such an endeavor may actually offer. And then what? Passé at twenty three?

Every child possesses a set of attitudes, beliefs and perceptions about themselves and their world. They should be encouraged to leave a written legacy to the future in their own words, which sheds a tiny light on who they were and why they believed they were here. What an impressive collection it would be, with all its foibles, errors and nonsense within an innocent expressiveness. Placed in time capsules or space capsules, their original thoughts and stories would be part of the future's landscape.

From cave dwellers' graphics, to written records, to high speed communications, people have always had something to say. Those in the past who were recorded were read and therefore had an impact and made a difference in and to their world. Their words lived on, after they were gone.

Today, virtually everyone has access to and can be recorded or documented in order that their words too may live on.
And why not? It sure beats "What I did on my summer vacation."

Branch Isole

Can't keep my eyes
from the circling sky
Tongue tied and twisted
just an earthbound misfit, I

America

Jamaican mon with blood 'O negative'
tests HIV positive
how long will he live?

Russian woman
abused and is beaten
her husband full of vodka
he has not eaten

Puerto Rican machismo
struttin' his stuff
Irish green
can't get enough

Scot's own whiskey
makes his lass frisky
Frenchman's escargot
he remembers Brigitte Bardot

The Lady a Celt
selling her pelt
Young man of Italia
in the contraband trade
Both work the street
dreams of 'being made'

Mexican Low Rider cruisin'
East African losin'
Lonesome Greek snoozin'
Native Indian boozin'

A melting pot
of simmer and sizzle
Stirred and
Mixed,
with human swizzle
sticks

Cars in garages
Chickens in pots
Reality TV to watch
"I'm not a have not"

The world's great 'Mulligan stew'
all Red
White
and Blue
Folks back home
if only they knew

Many here chasing
streets paved with gold
waiting and wondering
what next they'll be sold

The American Dream
The Cream of the Crop
Each, every and all
waiting their turn on top

And in their quest
for material bliss
New problems, yes
they do exist

Hurdles and sink holes
stumble and swallow
any and all who would
yet still wallow

A few will be prized
by wanton dreams
Most mesmerized
by survival scenes
The rest paralyzed
by human schemes

No way to hold back
the oncoming tide
of a questing humanity's
USA ride
From all the oceans
yet do they flow
Both joys and miseries
soon to be known . . .

For between the shores
of this mighty land
it is here
all believe,
"I can"

Anticipation

My heart stops each time the phone rings.
The catch in my breathing chokes
as I wait to hear your name identified out loud.

We've spoken and spat of our secret.
Proclaiming acknowledgement
of our lust's initial shared understanding.
Me insistent. You half-hearted.

Your insecure threats hang over me.
Their preponderance
as if a guillotine blade
prepared to be loosed,
waiting to cleave the momentary pause
between bouts of anticipation of you
and the guilt of a characterless vow
made to my spouse.

Revelation doggedly shadows
our movements in public.
Darting clandestinely, wondering,
if the entity which is us
will accidentally be exposed
by friends or acquaintances
from my other life.

You torture by innuendo
when we are apart
and tantalize with orifices
as we copulate.

You don't own me,
I proceed willingly
into the slavery
of your sexual proclivities

and yet

aware we have no future
our abuses continue.

Beast With Two Backs

The beast with two backs
came to my room last night

Unable to turn
from its mesmerizing sight
I watched it,
with frightful delight

Contorted
Confused
its fluids ran
splattered
and oozed

Over the sheets
onto the bed

Bathing completely
its four heads

Oh how I dreamed
wished and prayed

I too might be
swept away

To be one with its growl
howl and screams
Totally immersed
in its heated extremes

Both drawn to
and disgusted
by its gleaming skin
wondering,
should I join in?

Watching the performance
salivating on the show
a wink and a nod
to let me know
Then asking,
how far I'd like to go?

"Come"
the smiling beast said
"Come"
get on the bed
"Come"
let me have you too
"Come"
I'll consume all of you

I stood,
frozen in time
stepping forward
only in my mind

I sat,
fantasy dissolved
from the room
I wanted to crawl

"Wait,"
said the beast
"before you go
Answer me this
for I want to know"

"Shall we return
tomorrow night?
Or have you seen enough
of this carnal sight?"

Walking away
the scene continued to play
over and over
in my head,
the beast with two backs
wrestling on the bed

Wishing I had
afraid that I might
have become part
of that covetous sight

Birthday Wish

Another year past
This new one begins
Today we celebrate your birth

A special day
for all involved
Marking your appearance
that first distinct moment
you joined us here on earth

To be known by you
a blessing to share
as family and friends we sing

Our collective love
is heralded by
the joy for us
your presence brings

Happy Birthday ~

Blur

Snake-like movements
a gliding slither through the grass
Blurred line toward androgyny
the torch of distinction
passed in '63

Revolution, Evolution
Sparks of social commentary

Seedlings as innocuous
as Beatles' mop top hair
gave meaning to 'generation gap'
Youthful exuberance
called and labeled 'crap'

The search for truthful honesty
found in experimental art filled mediums
Lead to drugs and disco styles
expanding lives of tedium

Usury interest rates
to draw back upon the reigns
of social displaced priorities
Attempts at control to regain

Abandon truth and its pitiful search
Make thine enemy your own
Foe becomes friend easily
when enticed with enough
golden bones

Build a house of cards
Pyramid Scheme string along
Make millionaires of young and old
Robber barons of paper dot coms

Revolution
Evolution
Truth correction,
not this time
Probationary penalties
now fit the crime

Statements of solidarity
Arm in arm linked for strength,
not this time
An uneducated
insecure generation
emerging into its prime

No self respect
Absence of will
Personal and property damage
A revenge filled night's thrill
Insecure emotions fully ablaze
this time,
not a phase

New brotherhood
New sisterhood
Void of truth's veracity
yet brazenly over exposed
through self corrupted identity

Brothers in Arms

Brothers in form, in peace and in right
Brothers in life, in death from the fight
We would all be brothers in heart and might
If only we loved each other
with His Holy Light.

Carl's Bad Kid

He entered the courtroom
white as a ghost
Six months of confinement
county jailer his host
The charge was murder
in the first degree
Killed her son they said,
first step of a spree?

Hysteria reigned
that rainy morning
the son now dead
the mother in mourning

He denied the charges
proclaiming he loved her still
She had stood by him
married now, not against her will

Their fate to be decided
by twelve of his peers
Lethal injection one option
or perhaps twenty-five years?

A readied prosecution
all ducks in a row
The list of witnesses
one by one in tow

Her friends and relatives
ulterior motives each
To see this boy,
this boy from the beach
Tried, lied
and hopefully fried

One week went by
then number two
Now the defense
but what would they do?
What kind of defense
no one quite knew
Only one witness
for the boy
it was true

It would be up to the accused
to describe the scene
the one that took place
before he heard his wife scream

Nothing left to do
except tell the truth
That was to be
his only proof

"I thought it a dream
the ball beneath my back
until I realized
it was poor little Jack"

"Not really moving
but still ok
I left him to sleep
'til the break of day"

The forensics in
all opinions stated
Jury deliberations
the next day were slated

Back and forth
the arguments went
Guilty, not guilty
After eight hours
all jurors were spent

Fresh for a second day of talks
Outside in the hall
both attorneys did walk
Twelve votes seesawed
back and forth
Six yeas, six nays,
now eight and four

Adjournment once again
the weekend at hand
they'd reconvene Monday
to review the lay of the land

On the third day they voted
but to no avail,
tempers flared
discussions failed
Asking for transcripts
what had been missed?

Once again
they examined their list

Recounting stories told
by both sides involved
Surely the answer there
to this mystery be solved
The state's star witness
had left a clue
Overlooked by all
who should have knew

To gain peace and quiet
throughout the house
To escape the pressures
a hand over a mouth
Strain of the moment
of fury befitted
It became obvious . . .
the mother did it

Conversant

Lord, it has been so long since we've talked,
I wonder why that is

The peace you reveal
quiets all other clamorous desires
and transcendent attempts
to fill my heart
Yet it is not until I am here again
with you
I realize and remember

Understanding you are always available
it is I who become caught up
in the ways and means of my world

I awake to stare at the eyes in the mirror
seeing me, not you
with plans of the day ahead
and their impending struggles
As ominous as the unseen beast
waiting to spring from the shadows
to wrestle life away from me
Devouring my self importance
Draining the spirit coursing through my veins

As if a wanderer
bedazzled by the vibrant colors of the jungle
Myopically through its façade
a false sense of security prevails

Straying from the veneered path,
not until lost
do my trembling thoughts refocus upon you
as my pleadings begin
And there you are
reminding me,
be still
be calm
for I AM here

Evening arrives and my exhaustion is palatable
Reflections of disparaging events and offenses
occupy both mind and body
as my spirit cries out silently

Extricating myself from worries
which exert feigned control,
hoping that in dream
my soul might be recharged
once more by yours
A renewed communion of spiritual energy
as we were before

Dementia

I've written this
before. . .
I think

Desperate Pleadings

Gambler's wish
Numbers hit

Racer's need, speed
Never relinquish the lead

Pastor's plight
Attendance more
Sunday night

For each and every woman and man
in the heart
a success dream planned

a little more. . .
if only. . .
perhaps. . .

No possible failure
No ruinous collapse

Boom, no bust
Yes, a must
(please. . . .)

Detached Retina of Your Third Eye

You cat around
like a dog in heat
Giving the bird to all you meet
who wait to see you worm,
turn and squirm
You bleat foul words
accompanied by gestures of hands
conjured up to cut the throats
of your anointed sacrificial lambs

Lying in wait
you lionize your pride
Touting you're a leopard
who can change its spots
While others turn blind eyes
to your demeanor of disrepute
and egomaniacal behavior

Your clouded search
continuing daily
thought to be clearer
by the eyes of the mirror

Enabler

We think we are right
when we appease
with our efforts,
conversations
our attempts to please,
others and self
with misguided good
As if they needed
As if we should

We support what they say,
do
and expect
While we ourselves know
the ones we love
are once again headed
for an emotional train wreck

Why is it we shun
our knowledge of truth
As if we also
needed more proof
To stand up for right
once and for all
To stand straight
and direct them
from their impending fall

Repetition of failure
Of repeating the past
Failing to remember
the pain suffered last
A cycle never broken
only to be relived
and yet,
a cycle breaking answer
we fail to give

Where is the love
the well-being held tight?
Beneath our laugh
our symbolic denial
that all will be okay
As we and they
avoid the Truth,
one more day

Equalizers

Finally it's happened
At last it's been done
A humanity accomplishment
anticipated, waited on
long before century twenty-one

The great socio-economic equalizer
having arrived on man's scene
Rejoicing now
from the tops of our lungs
hear our fraternal
primal scream

From positions long held
by "have's" versus "have nots"
Separate, made equal now
merging egos, identities
moving up
moving down

Mayhem's modern equalizer
not one, but two;
Multi-tasking cell phones
and multiple tattoos

Father and Son

Observing a boy
hug his father today
Unlike you,
he did not turn away.

Watching, wondering
how for that young boy it felt
to receive a smile and contact
as his father knelt.

To receive and return
a love so freely given
When and Where was it
this father learned
to share with his son,
a sense of life
worth living

Fire Dancer

The heat
the smoke
the flames that dance
Around my feet
they gently prance
The searing pain
of burning flesh
All
put me to the test

Peeling back
layer upon layer
The explosive singe
of burning hair
Tied and bound
i do watch
As i become
a human torch

May i become
a radiant light
To show those caught
and trapped by the night
The justice reward
for sins not atoned
My soul now looking
for its new home

A home above
Below
or beneath
Or cast among the gnashing teeth
The moans
the groans
the wailing
and tears
forever is . . . how many years?

Alone
forgotten
and now to be tossed
Upon the heap
with others as lost

Separated
from Father
Son
and Holy Spirit
Your Gospel story
just once more
could i hear it?

This time i would listen
understand
and obey
The love and desires
of the One who did say

"I love you forever
and for one more day
If only you would have
chosen my Way"

"My Son did I send
that you each might know
There is but one path to follow
One way to go"

"To reach me once more
after all your trips
back and forth
that you might not miss"

"Your final escape
your final decision
your final choice
without rescission"

"With just one thought
one word
one deed
you could have shown
your true belief"

"Out of my love
I tried
and tried
And all you could do
was continue to lie"

"To lie, cheat and steal
is the world's common way
Its way of life
each day until decay"

"To murder
to covet
and to attack
Worse than all these
was to turn your back"

"On Me
on My Son
on My Spirit
My Love...
All
had been sent
for you from above"

i wouldn't listen, i wouldn't hear
the words which came to both my ears
Yes i heard but did not know
It was me in the balance
between above and below
It was, i thought . . . all about me
Not about He who hung on that tree
Taking my place once and for all
My ego now no longer stands tall

The me of this world now passing away
My soul all alone, wanting to stay
With you oh Lord, had i only obeyed

Forgiveness

Forget it,
I have.

Games

You,
the self proclaimed
Master
If they ever ask me
I'll answer,
Bastard

I haven't got time for your games
Not since you left me

You,
labeled them
'the Grand Dame Games'
As you chipped away
piece by piece,
heart
mind
body and soul
You required
a relinquishing of all
to be part of the ball,
Asshole

I haven't got room for your games
Not since you left me

You,
sweet talking
charmer
with deceit filled
quips
and one liners
Passionate Marquis de Sade
complete with chains
and whips,
Prick

I haven't the mood for your games
Not since you left me

You,
two timer
three
four, maybe more
Stringing each along
a bevy of beauties
in your throng,
Son of a Bitch

I haven't the need for your games
Not since you left me

You,
lying there
in your own fluids and waste

How do you feel now?
where is your smile?
your coy sneer?
oh how sad,
I'm glad
your face is smeared,
blood red
from the bullet hole
in your head

I haven't got time for your games
I haven't got room for your games
I haven't the mood for your games
I haven't the need for your games
Not since you left me

goodbye
forever
this time,
Cocksucker

No
no, no
no more of your games,
Now that you've left me

Good Until

Have you ever imagined
what might be
the very last thing
you'll ever see

The terminally ill
grapple with this thought
but what about you,
what about me

Aren't we also
slated to die
To pass away
while wondering why

If you possessed foreknowledge
of your last moments
here on earth,
would you spend your time
waiting and watching
or contemplating your worth

Did you contribute
something good,
such as love
and service
Or were you consumed
with desires of self and indulgence

Busy modern lives
afford no time
for such philosophical
profundities
We are much too involved
with our own little needs
to grapple with the questions
of eternity

As for me
I never worry
if death will be coming
early or late,
my birth certificate came
with an expiration date

Guilt

I walk this path
struggling
Waiting on you to keep your word
your promise
Then, recognizing your guarantee
never included fulfilling my dream

Straw man of my own fabrication
A bait and switch maneuver
of my own making,
egged on by you
as if forgiveness
its own reward
for abstinence and denial

Yet I dare not test
the bounds of self
For the consequences
may drive me mad
through guilt

Having outgrown shame
and its damaging public repercussions
realizing now,
you don't need me
to glorify you

that is my need

in order to
validate a reason beyond self
for success
should it ever come to pass,
and to vilify failure
when it takes its place
atop the pedestal of embarrassment
and upon the platform of degradation

for not surrendering my dream
in exchange for yours

H_ng m_n

How well kn_wn are we?
At wh_t point cel_brity?
Effo_ts in our wor_d, lon_evity?
Desir_us r_sults, l_sting le_acy?
L_a_n _o r_a_
Qui_ _es_e_tial _cti_ity
E_pre_s_ _l_w_ _ te
lac a_d _h_ _e
_ _l in p_ai_ s_ght
Hidd_n behi_d s_oke and mir_ors!
M_de to mag_cally r_appear!
Out fr_m the sh_dows!
Off to the gall_ws!

Has Been

On the road
without a roadie
Lights and electronics
fall to,
the Fallen Star

Back to the beginning
To that lonely land
of the willing
Back again
without top billing

Name
no longer in lights
nor on boulevard marquee
Now no longer a flower,
once again
a weed

Sowing in a field
of edgy new listeners
Paying with heart
and soul
Seeing their neck hairs
starting to bristle
Young eyes stare
as if she's too old

Trying
to make the grade
in a scene
already made
Away but for
a matter of months
Forgotten quickly
without media punch

Kissing the asses
of self aggrandized punks
Their musical awareness
fits in two lumps
Struggling to re-establish
after a few mistakes
How much more
of her soul
will they take?

These are the costs
and dues to be paid
for once more the chance
to get her music played

In the Wake

We mourn not for the loss of life
but for the life that was
and is no more
The depth of our investiture
reminds us
of our own mortality
Our dear departed one
whispers to us
"Don't cry for me."

"We shall no longer share
a moment's experience together
until we meet once more
and you shall be guided
by blessing and spirit
into worlds unknown"

"Look each of you
at the collective gathered here
Mourn in my stead for each other,
for the one
into whose eyes you stare
at revealed fear and grief
masking personal disbelief"

We glimpse our own loss
A realization we encounter
at death's expense of another

For one day we too shall be gone
from this familiar place,
our little space
in this human race

And what are we racing to
or from?
Only the soul knows
the spirit's journey
along the path

It is our soul that mourns

Influences

Some say
it's DNA
Others claim
it's just the way
The way it is
from environs near and far
That make us do
what we do
That make us who
we truly are

The way we're raised,
silver spoon
or rougher
often determines
how much we suffer

All come naked into the world
pure and virginal
caught up in the swirl
Of turmoil and trouble
none will escape
All will be pummeled
pounded and raped
Some raped of body
others of mind,
all beaten
all bruised,
different types
different kinds

And what can change
the way we grow
What can remedy the ebb, the flow
of who we become
are
or will be
How are we ever
set totally free?
From the dastardly things
we had to experience
as children, as youth
caught up in delirious
Ways of the world
which torture and scour
our souls, our minds
each year, day and hour

Condemned to try
to live by umber and unction
in families
in groups
full of dysfunction

To where can we turn,
hide
or come forward
In what state of being,
courageous or coward

What is it that influences
above all others

Over siblings
fathers
even our mothers

Is it TV ?
Or money ?
Or jobs
we'd like to shove ?
No,
It's simply the abundance
or the lack
of love

It's A Crime

My gang colors
are blue and cammo
We're bad ass mother fuckers
and carry plenty of ammo

When we're on the block
or in the hood,
citizens know
to be acting good

No one threatens
jokes or cajoles us
We don't put up with bullshit
back talk
or whiner's fuss
We don't give a damn
what you may think
We honestly believe
"our shit doesn't stink"

We do exactly what we want
and on the streets do we flaunt
our guns, our muscle
and our screw you
attitude

Night or day when we show up
it's always in full force
We take for ourselves
what we want
after breaking down your doors

Born and bred
to entrap
We never take
only dish out the crap

Yes,
there are psychos in our ranks
sociopaths and losers
in both flanks
but we're brothers in arms
and partners in scams
We set up walls
for any brother being jammed

Don't test or cross
our thin blue line
or you may find yourself
accused of a crime

So go ahead
get good and mad

Who cares?!

We're the ones
with the guns
and the badge

"To Protect & Serve"

Jezebel

Sure, she's smiling
to your face
so you won't notice the daggers
set in place,
behind selfish eyes

Turn your back
once too often
give an inch
or an ounce
she'll measure you
and upon you trounce

she'll use you
abuse you
disregard you
discard you

break your spirit
no regrets,
that's exactly
what to expect

For she is the Queen
of all she surveys
and in her game
if you want to play,
with your heart
or your soul you'll pay

Spiked tongue
hands and feet
ready to swing into action
Rest assured
upon your back
she'll claw for traction

Ripping flesh
Digging deep
into raw
and bloodied meat

Pillaged, plundered
mentally scarred
damage complete

She believes nothing can
or ever will
bring her down
No way she'll give up
her imagined tiara crown
nor her self perceived reign
over this small town

she'll abuse you
use you
discard you
disregard you

break your spirit
no regrets,
that's exactly
what to expect

Ask her,
She'll show you
tell you
give you proof
Only miscalculation
in her grand scheme,
the arrival and presence
of death's waiting truth

Last Ride

Life in a world
of quasi vanity
Altered states
of relative sanity

How to fill
the void of time
on this lonesome trip
A stowaway's journey
in the grasp and hold
of this flesh and blood
tethered ship

Captain
of this small craft
Adrift,
No draft
for this lonely life raft

Cast ashore
on rock number three
Mind, soul, body
and me

Sailing vessels
moored and tied
their vast numbers still untold
Patiently awaiting appointed release
out with the ebb
in with the flow

Gliding as a vapor trail
above the rising tide
one last trip . .
this last journey . . .
my last voyage . . . .
life's last ride

Letters

Dear God,

You put us in
this selfish place
Controlling species
our human race

Full of Temptations
Choices
Deadly sins
We love filling
our hearts
with them

Refusing responsibility
for outcomes different
than pre-conceived

Fighting for celebrity
today one's name
is the game

Oh hallelujah
to be like you God
where everyone knows
who you are,
number one
most famous
the biggest
the best,

known by all
more than all the rest

You can't hold me responsible
for all the mistakes I've made
You're to blame
for me being as I am
by the way

You gave me choices
and freedoms to decide
which outlandish
lame excuse to use
as my next lie,
I'm here struggling
trying to get by

P.S. Yes I know
It's been a while,
since I've thought of you
Longer still
since we last talked
A lifetime if the truth be told
from when our spirits
were interlocked

P.P.S. And Lord
just one more little thing
Now that you know
I'm still here
Send more money
if it pleases you,
a Vegas jackpot or lottery will do

Love's Child

no one who experienced
unconditional love as a child
can ever become a poet

Massage Me

Massage my heart with love
Massage my mind with ideas and thoughts
Massage my emotions with understanding
and compassion
Massage my body in all the right places
Massage my psyche without ration

Massage my heart with love
from here as well as from up above

Massage my mind with ideas and thoughts
that the bulb may shine
bright and hot

Massage my emotions with understanding
and compassion
so when times are tough
roads are rough
and nothing ever appears enough,
provide me with strength
to repel and rebuff

Massage my body in all the right places
that each sensation
leaves permanent traces
Massage my psyche without ration
that the adult
who has grown
from free inner child
may still be inquisitive
and a little bit wild

Muse

For the artist
the writer
and especially the poet,
a Muse is essential

For some it is practicum
For others it be spiritual
For all indeed
it's application, mental

A point of inspiration
A happening
within a nation

An observation
of life's eternal struggle
and wonder

A relationship
lifted on high
Or one
ground asunder

A pinpoint of light
in the darkness
Darkness of a black hole
lost in space
Any or all
may be the Muse,
For few it's in the mirror's face

love and hatred
death and life
childhood in young or old
mistress, wife

dichotomies all
throughout time
play upon the poet's
rational,
irrational
seasoned mind

Is the artist
the writer
or especially the poet
aware of the Muse?
Or is it the Muse,
the Muse...
who truly knoweth?

Who controls the brush
the pen
the paper, the pad
Poet's mind or Poet's hand?
Or the one who waits
and lives
in Muse's distant land

My Generation

It's often been said
our past stays with us
through thick and thin
but if you look closer
surely you'll see
how much change
there's actually been

My generation is different
Our WASPY world now open
to all beliefs
stripes
and persuasions
Now an equal opportunity land
for every person or occasion

From the old ways
of then
to the new ways
of now,
Not that they've earned it
Nor do they deserve it
but no longer do we force
or demand they kowtow

My generation is different
from those here before
No longer do we slam shut
opportunity's now open door

Today we're accepting
of all people
all kinds
Even when they cause trouble
or make life a grind

My generation is different
Not a prejudice bone
do we have
in our collective white body
We ain't against anyone of 'em,
we don't burn 'em
turn 'em, harass 'em
blast 'em or hang 'em,
hell,
we don't even treat 'em shoddy

My father and his,
told and showed me
what's needed to promote
the white man's good
They thought and taught
it was accomplished
by wearing
a white sheeted hood

My generation is different
we don't try to keep 'em out
the micks
the spics
the wops
the kikes
the nigs and all da kine
The only hood
my generation wears
is the one that covers
our collective closed minds

None So Blind

much of life
is anticipation of change,
as the stumbling blocks
which drag on the present
appear to fade
into the shadows
cast by the neo light of
Potential

in actuality
they are camouflaged
by distractions,
becoming disassociative disruptions
to the enlightenment of
Future

we run
but cannot hide,
our sojourned trip continuing

expecting elation
we experience disappointment

for freedom exists
and is nurtured only by
the reality of Truth

Omnivision

There are unseen eyes
watching each of us
from near yet oh so far

Tears are shed
droplets of sorrow
for pains suffered yesterday
today and tomorrow

Other glares
are of disgust
for actions of greed
and self-centered lust

With omnipresent sight
He sees all of these
and every single possibility
In each heart
In each mind
Into each reality

God's unseen eyes
see all there is
of every living thing
Nothing escapes His view
Not the ancient
Not the new

Omniscient
compassion, understanding, forgiveness. . .
why is it
so many people need these three
and instead for self, put them aside

We may believe
we have hidden in the darkness
of heart and mind,
our sinful mistakes
all judgment errors,
yet in truth
there is no valid excuse
for our disobedient acts

Without His omnipotent love
and guiding sight
Day would never
have evolved from night
Safety would be
obscured by fright
and mankind would not know
His Holy Light

We hope and pray
He may not know
not one will He find out
but those unseen eyes
which see all there is
and ever now have been,
lovingly wait
for us to look
finally seeing Him

Paradise Portals

Through these portals
they do proceed
CEO's and their nannies
auto workers
Avon sales ladies
grandpas with grannies

Having arrived in paradise
as if children their first time at Disneyland
some walk single file
others stroll hand in hand

One leads
One doesn't hear
The blind leading the deaf
Dazed
by three hundred sixty degree sights
Without a thought
of what is near

No idea
of what to expect
deluge of visitor information
has left them a wreck

Where to next?
What now can we do?
Sit and rest please
with shopping
I'm through

I can't go on
I won't
I refuse

No more
no more
spending abuse

our credit card numbers
no longer bas relief
razed by excessive use

"Ok honey,
I'll be right there"

Printed in Red

To your name I shriek
crying aloud,
please steal me away
from this madden crowd

Of all the books
upon which I have fed
it's your simple words
printed in red
That fills the longings
of my soul
That fills with love
my life's empty whole

The world I've known
takes care of me
keeps me chained
so fervently
keeps me fixated
upon its gold,
buys me
sells me
makes me grow old
It's your simple words
printed in red
That fills the emptiness
in my head

From here
to there
and back again
slipping in and out
from sword and pen
Whom to trust
Whom to believe
They all speak
so eloquently

It's your simple words
printed in red and set apart
That fills the void
within my heart

This day they be friends
next generation foes
From this time to that
who really knows
Feed 'em
Fight 'em
Forget 'em

and so it goes,
and so it goes

My turning from your love
to Satan's graft
keeps my feet
upon this world's path

It's the merit of my actions
causing me this dread,
not your simple words
printed in red

Remembrance

Loving you the way I do
why is it I feel such a fool

You led me on
made me feel strong
Provided surety
over insecurity

Discovering now it was all a lie
Stage props, each time you tried
Deceit your way
Pulling heartstrings, you did play
Tempting me
as if fine wine
Your intentions from the start
to leave me to crying

Now you're gone, I'm alone
I'd take you back despite the pain
Knowing once more
the sorrow you'd cause
Assured one more time
my heart you would cross

How could you have been
so cold
so bold
Days with and without you
a living hell

Your hell
I would gladly accept
if together once more we slept
To feel your touch
caress your skin
In my deluded heart
we both would win

Sailor's Garden

From a long line of agrarians
came a seafaring Aquarian
A farmer at heart
Tall ship, his cart

Tiller in hand
sailing land to new land
His life spent at sea
navigating world round
to port after port
and town after town

At each global place
and every new space
in mound upon mound
did he plow new ground

Longing to be used
for temporary gardening
in pockets at sea
his tools had been hardening

Recounting once more
from long ago past
Recalling sea stories
how to make it last

Excavating fresh ground
each deep furrowed new mound
Pale red dearth
pink, supple and sweet
waiting to bear fruit
mind and body complete

Working his hoe
day and night
watching and waiting
this new mound now ripe

He said it is here
in this mound I shall stay
for in this rich moisture
I desire to play,
as a bulbous hood
was plied softly away

Remembering lonely nights at sea
when it was hands on the mast
All efforts now languid
not going too fast

From this seaman
came seeds
which he had brought
in his pulsating quiver
full,
bulging
and hot

Using his tool
each portal received
all efforts to please
one final release

Shuddering acceptance
Long furrow lain
Slow strokes back and forth
Sun's trek was now stayed

Sun once more dawning
Sailing visitor did sow
Receiver of life's seed
now gloriously aglow

Using his hoe
in this warmth he did know
the taste of sweet fruit
from one local grove

Awaiting rekindling of his planting desire
stoking flames to recreate intensity's fire
He would once more a furrow plow
filling her ripe and ready bowels
with bursting buds of husbandry
before returning to the sea

Alas however, it was not to be
Watching tearfully
he slipped back to the sea

Her sailing farmer
and his ship so tall
neither to return
until the next fall

Now is the garden
eager and willing
to receive her sailor
for more rapturous tilling
For when he returns
all brush be removed
for where once was
but barren ground,
now a rich and moist
fertile mound
doth abound

Silver Streak

From out of the night sky
it came
From a galaxy
yet to be named
Streaking through
the black abyss
Collision course
a celestial body to hit
From across the light years
Space traveler, how far have you come?

Skin Deep

Medical data retrieval
sounds innocent enough
Offer it for free
they'll all line up

A tiny Microchip
oh so thin,
planted
just beneath the skin
Ply them with guilt responsibility
every woman and man
Explain it will help find
those lost, abandoned

Market it
like a wanton tattoo
Having one will make you hip;
"you'll be so hot,
so cool"

Update the data
annually,
free of charge
Offer frequent flyer miles
or green stamp points
to be saved and used
to buy that new car

Make it a sin
or a crime,
a highly embarrassing shame
To be last on your block
walking around
without a registered microchip name

Then when it's time
to be scanned and checked
for the Mark of the Beast
all will be pre-assigned,
subcutaneously

Sleeping With You

When sleep whispers
and calls to me
I always go willingly
For it is there
the two of us meet
to renew our mutual
fantasy

Most often 'tis only we
you and me,
as we wrestle in the heat
basted by love's juices
complete

Then overwhelming desires
to share and fulfill each other
gently enters peripherally
A word, a wink, a nod,
an understood mutuality
Together
each surrenders
Attempts one, to the other to please
once more
yes, more,
than ever before

Stoking excitement's flame
the continued thrill of infatuation
alive and burning
fanned by lust,
on the embers of commitment
and total trust

Gently and openly
sharing vulnerabilities
and secrets for one another

Risking to take love
higher and higher
Testing the limits of our desires

Sharing wholly
individual thoughts and fantasies
Learning where they cross and meet
coming together,
as do we

for CC

Soul Resignation

World's design
stimulus,
ergo
response

Past regrets
Future's fear unknown
Today's besiegement
Seeds of control
in conflicts sewn

Mind's design
Physical desire
Soul's respite
flesh and bone soon to retire

All work completed
All races run
All tasks depleted,
accomplishments done?
accomplishments none.

He who dies
with or without
still does he die
Spirits fly
Bodies cry
Minds query
wondering why

Words resound
Lessons taught
Examples shown
Fellowship sought

The way He walked
The things He did
The legacy He left

What was His purpose?
According to who's plan?
Where leads the path
that recaptures the man

Spurned Ex-es

Woke up this morning,
took a shit,
thought of you

Surely "O"

Believing her role
demands a duty
of honor and respect
'Tis true she understands
the concept
Yet something deep within
makes her comprehend
mistakenly,
it is a role
cloaked in love

Love and worthiness
To her the same
Two separate yet equal parts
in life's acting game

Requited love
she desperately needs
to prove to herself existentially
Value and worth
neatly tied and bound
Attached to and circumscribed
As depicted in the roles
and titles,
Mother
Parent

Never knowing
realizing or understanding
Respect is earned,
Honor bestowed. . .

and Indifference
is the opposite of love

Tempered Temptations

A weighted shard of ragged edged molten metal
The cast iron wedge of the world
is driven into the heart of the believer
with each compelling nuance
to become one with God

Peace disrupted
Satan's ranks laugh at our inept attempts
to declare allegiance to our Lord
They bow down to the one
who,
with a mere waggle of his finger
draws nigh those on the precipice point
balancing self and selfless

They laud his presence and persistence
knowing condemnation awaits
yet to bask momentarily with him
in his temporal glory
over one of God's own
is worth every minute of eternal damnation

How strong is such a force
that all material sins bend to honor him
and yet to do battle
on our own behalf
all we are given is free will to choose

The Saint

Self; his code word
Insecurity his banner
His treatment of you well observed
Actual love and affection
far removed from his manner

Outwardly he could appear
so dear and respecting
but behind closed doors
and on occasion
in front of others
From the crack in his armor
escaped the shadow of the harmer

Your heart had known for many a year
you even made amends
His verbal abuse intended to break
yet all you did, was bend

As you used love
He used control
as only he could do
You did your best
and he did his
Now all of that is through

The same old games
the ones he played
with and on your heart
Your denial then
Your denial now
not so far apart

Then,
His behavior, made you think twice
Now,
Please recall, he wasn't that nice
Then,
was filled with your hidden pain
Now,
the drops which dampen your eyes
come only from rain

The rest knew
Could certainly see
The stress and hurt
he caused you
As you were held hostage
by your words, "I do"
Prisoner,
of marital captivity

Yes,
there was a committed bond
both exciting and sublime
What started out in lust and desire
ended in emotional ruin
eroded by passing time

Broad brush strokes
of need and self
On his life's canvas
did he paint

No longer lonely
Now you are free
Portray him not now
to be a saint

The Traveler

I once saw an image
of Buddha
in Buda,
Texas
on a trip to see
one of my ex-es.
Then on a journey
to Wichita Kansas
I met a girl
from Port Aransas
Said she was trying
to get back home
but that she was actually
from Nome,
Alaska.
We traveled together
as far as Reno
where we met a lady
who liked to play Keno
The first one left
the second one stayed
and for about a week we played,
Black Jack.
I won a little
but soon lost my shirt
then met a woman
who liked to flirt,
a lot.
She asked me to join
her and her friend
and so we began

to party hardy
with a case of rum
labeled Bacardi
until I awoke,
and found myself in Denver
no joke, Colorado.
Next off to Aspen
to get some skiing in
it's there I met
a great new friend,
She was a killer,
No, really,
She was on the lamb
wanted for a murder
in Birmingham,
Alabama
down south,
and could she ever use her mouth
Trash talker, you understand
even so she could also use her hand,
for hitch hiking.
We hit it off right away
said I was the first guy she'd met
along the way
who wasn't gay,
We licked
and frolicked
all night one day
then decided to part and separate
guess it was always our predestined fate.
She went West
and I went North,
Dakota

Then caught a ride to Minnesota,
Ya!
Learned they have 10,000 lakes
each with resident mosquitoes
make no mistake,
I became a feast
for a couple of weeks.
Decided to get
'on the road again'
as Willie Nelson
would say,
Hitch hiked all the way
to Florida
on the I-75 freeway corridor.
Landed in West Palm
with a new pair of shades on
Looking the part
met an Aussie bartender
who liked to play darts.
She was a knockout
that was for sure
and oooooooooh,
how she could purr,
like a raw v-8
motor, you know
for days and nights
man could she go
Revved me up
and round
and round,
rubbed my little nub
right into the ground,
I recovered

eventually
but by then she was gone
Maybe back to the land of Oz
I wondered.
Cared not, for South Florida much
So went all the way to the home of the Dutch
Amsterdam you see,
from the states I wanted to flee.
So now I'm traveling,
by train
on my way to southern Spain,
Iberian Peninsula.
Think I'll stop there
to spend more time
drink some sangria
with a floating lime,
in the glass.
The Spaniards are nice people
so I've heard
an easy place to live
free as a bird
Have chosen either Barcelona,
Malaga
or perhaps Marbella
Understand rich ladies are there
who like to cavort on the Playa,
Del Sol.
One way or the other
believe I'll stop in
to visit my mother,
She lives there,
in Spain that is.

Things To Do Today

electrician crosses
two wires together
news anchor agrees
to report the weather

grocery store checker
asks the bag boy
one more time
police department snitch
drops one more dime

roller coaster operator
gives people
their first thrill
tax man sends
a past due bill

volunteer fire chief
rescues a kitten
from up a tree
Superman saves
Lois and Jimmy

elementary school teacher
explains basic math skills
despondent employee
enters the office
to kill

radio DJ
plays the same eight songs
and six commercials
all day,
farm boy wants
a roll in the hay

government official
takes another bribe,
and lies
oncologist looks
into another pair of eyes,
and lies

airline pilot
prepares to fly
terrorist highjacker
prepares to die

vacationer takes
a pictorial shot
teens toke
a little pot

artist creates,
toll booth attendant
raises a gate

butler and maid
keep on waiting
fishermen
keep on baiting

restaurateur
hires a new chef
eight year old
learns a new word
beginning with "F"

alcoholic takes
another drink of rum
car pooling soccer mom
swigs water with her Valium

Hollywood stripper
takes off her clothes
six year old
with the flu
blows his nose

municipal court judge
levies another fee
mafia muscle
breaks another knee

stockbroker cheats
yet another client
prison inmate
remains totally defiant

record producer dreams
of a number one
school yard bully
has his fun

these are
but a few
of the millions
of tasks
both old and new
on today's lists of,
Things To Do

Third Person Singular

A friend of mine was taken ill today
one day he'll be taken even farther away
Caught between each, body and mind
exists the One who has lived for all time

The essence of being
who lived with the Light
traveled the darkness
pierced the night

Finding anew a new spot to dwell
a transient place betwixt heaven and hell
Third Person of this spiritual existence
joins together mind and body
without initial resistance
A new life of joy
trials, tribulations and tests
Decisions and choices before final rest
Along the treacherous path
good times and bad,
compassion and wrath

Genderless being of eternal spirit
Third Person watcheth and intently heareth
the conversation
which mind has to say
as body slips further into decay

"Give me rest,
I've done my best"
cries out body's punished flesh
"I'm nowhere near ready
to leave this place
I've just now started
to understand its pace"
retorts now knowing mind
"Realizing the cost
of gain against loss
I'm in need
of a little more time"

Conflict persists
Third Person waits
Aware examination,
exemption
both wait at the gate

Assigned a task
of eternal immunity
Disguised by a mask
of temporary impunity

Mind and Body
drift further apart
Less and less stress,
Now a flat lining chart
Once more
Third Person free,
to stand again
before the Trinity

Mind knew of life
and so too with Body
Third Person's role
the duty of soul,
to bring together
once and for all
three standing anew
never again to fall

for Terry,
a gentle man and a gentleman

Thus Sayeth the Lord

In lieu of each drop of blood we've shed
with each drop of ink we've added
through the markings we freely desired
The Lord bequeaths
to you and me,
one day each
with the objects of our devoted
pictorial idolatry

For you with the rose
it will be rosy,
except for those thorns
penetrating your soul
For the ones with dragons
or wild animals assorted
it may not be cozy
with the carnivorous cavorting

For inked Christians
their sins atoned,
yet they too will be accountable
before the throne,
where God
will mete out
His justice great
in light of His Word
Leviticus,
Nineteen: twenty-eight

Tourist Trapped

Hawking their wares in the tourist trade
Each customer asks, "Is this Hawaiian made?"
"Or just another cheap imitation
coming here
from some third world nation?"

"But of course dear buyer,
Would I sell you goods
that would make me a liar?"

"I saw this same item
at 'Trash 'n Trinkets Galore'
you know,
that little 'Front Street' store"

"Those could not have been ours
we deal in only the finest
nothing in here
from Malaysia or China"

"I could swear this one appears
to be the same
It even has
the same label and name
The only thing I see, in glancing quicker
there is no 'made in the Philippines' sticker"

"Oh no, not us
No,
Never
Never
Every item we sell is authentic leather
Not Naugahyde, not vinyl
certainly no imitations
Those items never
get past immigration!"

"So these are originals
hand made right here,
yes?"

"Without a doubt
You can put me to the test,
I'll guarantee these are the best
far better than all the rest"

"Ok, let me try it
and I'll make my decision
One last choice
without revision"

"It doesn't seem to fit
like my regular size
Perhaps it's these tired
vacation eyes
Or I may have
holiday amnesia,
but the tag inside says
made in Indonesia"

Wasteland

Of all the entertainment
broadcasts that bore
two of the worst
have got to be;
celebrity poker
and Reality TV
scripted, as seen

Whale's Tale

We swim the depths
of the deep blue sea
My calf,
Others of the pod
and me

South from Alaska
Southwest are we bound
Four thousand miles
to the winter waters
of Old Lahaina town

Winters in mid-Pacific
each year
Summers in Alaskan waters
cool and clear

Our ancestors were hunted
after travel and toil
For scrimshaw bone
and burnable oil
We too today
pursued by many a man
No longer harpoons
now it's cameras in hand

Humpback's all
That's what we be
Our whale's tale of life
In the deep blue sea

Other books by Branch Isole

Postcards from the Line of Demarcation ©
Points of Separation in Poetic Prose
ISBN 0-9747692-6-6

Reflections on Chrome ©
Parking Lot Confessions in Poetic Prose
ISBN 0-9747692-5-8

Seeds of Mana'o ©
Thoughts, Ideas and Opinions in Poetic Prose
ISBN 0-9747692-1-5

Barking Geckos ©
Stories and Observations in Poetic Prose
ISBN 0-9747692-2-3

God. . .i believe ©
Simple Steps on the Path
of Spiritual Christianity ™
ISBN 0-9747692-0-7

Order books at www.manaopublishing.com
Questions, Comments; go to our website
and click on the 'contact' link.

MANA'O PUBLISHING
Home of the VOYEURISTIC POET

Living on the island of Maui, Branch Isole is the 'voyeuristic poet' who shares Mana'o* and God's Word in writing and with individuals and groups visiting Hawaii.

Branch also writes poetry, articles and short stories for journals, magazines, newsletters and on the Internet at www.manaopublishing.com

*Mana'o (pronounced Ma Na O) is Hawaiian for 'Thoughts, Ideas and Opinions'.